As We Are

Nancie Rees

authorHOUSE®

AuthorHouse™ UK
1663 Liberty Drive
Bloomington, IN 47403 USA
www.authorhouse.co.uk
Phone: 0800.197.4150

Published by AuthorHouse 01/16/2015

ISBN: 978-1-5049-3586-9 (sc)
ISBN: 978-1-5049-3587-6 (e)

This book is printed on acid-free paper.

Contents

Acknowledgements

I write poetry through my inspirations of experience and like to be able to relate with my audience of day to day life and share with you my expression.

I would like to say, Thank-you to my family and friends for their Support throughout the years and encouraging me to write this Book and Thank-You to Mrs B. J Smith and AuthorHouse for making this Book possible.

My faith is to support those who are less unfortunate than myself and to support for world peace. In Love for our people and the world that we share.

In Remembrance of my Late Mother Millicent. T. Beynon.

With Love & Regards

N Rees xxx

A Glimpse

The sunset skies
Colourful, bright,
As the moon appears
On a November night.

Dark blue and grey
All around,
As the coldness settles near,
The timing is bound.

The waters reach inward
They catch the glow,
In the distance
As we watch from below.

Beautiful, we watch
As it disappears,
A memory on a photograph
Throughout the years.

Glimpses we capture
Natural world unknown,
Therapeutic, calm
Our skies in pure tone.

The World We Live In

Such beautiful scenery
We have around the world,
Mountains and rocks
Sea and the fields.

Photographs are taken
Art pictures are drawn,
That's all we have left
Of this beautiful world.

What's happened to nature?
Most wild animals extinct,
Bombs being dropped
Our Children so lonely, Poor little things.

Nobody notices
Nobody cares,
Just carry on fighting
Putting on dares.

If only fighting
Could be so rare,
We would not have to live
In a terrible nightmare.

The shadows on a distance of waters
Deep, loneliness grasped
shrieking their bones be.
Darkness falls as air fire covers blue skies,
Dignity falls, personality gone.
Justifying every second that flew by
Lost, bewildered on solid ground. Sanity
Shot, minds almost there,
out on the frontline.
Closely sniped, their friends,
they bereaved a loss.

Deceived by their sight in all that they bare,
A battle underway, far, far away.
Day lasts forever with courage,
gripping teeth,
Bracing their persons for time that they stay.
Harshness hits as terror is obey. War
They faced, taunts they despair.
For Our Country

Sonnet

A darkened room
Is all it seems,
No daylight forms
A life once beamed.

Awaiting linen
Lay in a chair,
Cups on the table
Going nowhere.

The clock just chimes
His loneliness deep,
Not even a whisper
Only tears that weep.

Little effort he makes
Now lost all he had,
Holding his memories
At present are sad.

If only, If only
For his mind repeats,
The loss of his, Darling
Gone forever to retreat.

A Shadow On The Water

It filled the sky with colour
It shone brightly like the sun,
A shadow on the seabed
As it glowed for everyone.

It came down to earth so very slow
It was so beautiful to see,
Amazingly big, enormous
Photographs taken by you and me.

It rose up in the evening
Upon a summers night,
To watch the birds fly past it
It was a wonderful sight.

It is a part of nature
A part of the world at its best,
Watching it go down
As it became less and less.

It is fabulous our sunset
It makes us stand and stare,
A beautiful, colourful sky
Vibrant, ever so fare.

When The World Unfolded

It was when a volcano erupted
When the lave flow like a stream,
The heat took all in its path
Listening to the people scream.
But the earth stood still

A tornado hit a country
In full force it took control,
Making nothing but debris
Only news left, untold.
But the earth stood still

When an earthquake made its target
Tearing everything in sight,
Nobody safe within its reach
Leaving everyone scared at night.
But the earth stood still

The sun made fires in woodlands
Taking days to put them out,
Nothing could be warned to stop it
The world that took a clout.
But the earth stood still

Our world in all its glory
The silence as it unfolds,
Showing us what it can do
For all that has been told.
But the earth stood still

Having fun on the beach
Enjoying the sun,
Bathing and swimming
The joy has begun.

Off to the bar
To order some drinks,
Family awaiting,
My body. It sinks.

I thought I was dreaming
Panic became one,
Barely I had rushed back
Through mayhem, just done.

Closer it came
Only fear that I face,
Everyone running
My Family, No Trace.

I got out, I got out
I was lucky to survive,
That damn tsunami
Took so many lives.

IN REAL LIFE

In This Life

There is so much we have
In this world today,
A lot less greed and understanding
Would go a long way.

Why all the fighting
When the world is to share,
Wouldn't it be nice
If there were, no crosses to bare.

Love, peace and respect
Is what we all need,
Take care of each other
Our Children indeed.

This concrete jungle we're in
There is so much to choose,
Much more options are open
We don't have to live in a bin.

We just need to be happy
Don't have to be a star,
Just enjoy our lives
Enjoy who we are.

Nature

In touch with nature
That we understand,
Birds and the butterflies
Land on the ground.

Beautiful colours
All types to see,
Wonderful creatures
Some not retrieved.

Ants, Bees and Spiders
Doing their best,
To feed their families
The ones in the nests.

Approaching the flowers
Nectar they seek,
Through the lens of a camera
The effects are meek.

Caring of nature
The beauty we need,
All around the world
It starts from a seed.

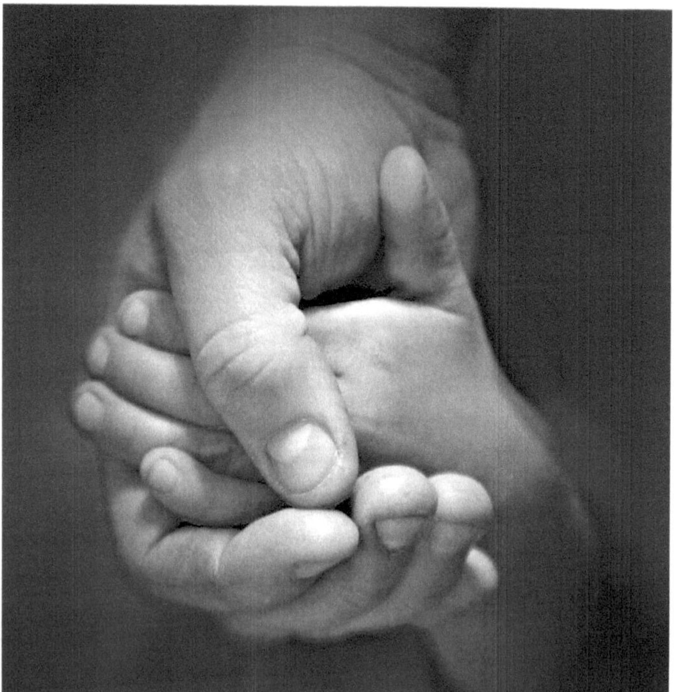

Wake up one morning
A part of us gone,
Feeling so vulnerable
What can be done?

Our little angels
No more do we see,
Only letters by post
That is all, it's to be.

Sets of depression
Their emotions are right,
But after they're taken
There's no way to fight.

Our Children's emotions
The long-term effects,
Drifted a part
Questions and Regrets.

Families are lost
It's so hard to move on,
After our angels,
Our family has gone.

This is supporting the families who lose their Children through Adoption 2014.

Departure

Earthquakes and volcanos
Erupting all around,
Storms and Hurricanes
Breaking many homes.

No more laughter
We hear in the town,
Such saddened faces
Not much sound.

Trying to find loved ones
Amongst the rubble,
Everyone helping
In all of their troubles.

Putting out fires
Burying their dead,
Carrying on, with their lives
Frightened to go to bed.

Rebuilding their lives
With nothing to show,
We are so lucky
That much I know.

As We Are

For here are we
In a world to share,
Strangers to each other
But we care.

Go about our lives
Day to day,
Looking for new goals
A long the way.

Our emotions, our feelings
Guide us on our path,
Experiences of others
We follow in mass.

Happiness, love
We each have in our hearts,
Reaching out, touching
So we do not part.

Beings, Individuals
All of Mankind,
In search of better
As we are, we each find.

Anchor Head

The wave's crash
Against the rocks,
The wind begins to howl,
At Anchor Head.

The sunset blooms
The sky changes form,
Relaxing moments,
At Anchor Head.

The chairs outside
The café full,
Enjoying the scenery,
At Anchor Head.

The seagulls fly over
They perch on the wall,
Catching their breath,
At Anchor Head.

The sun is out
The sky is grey,
A busy day
At Anchor Head.

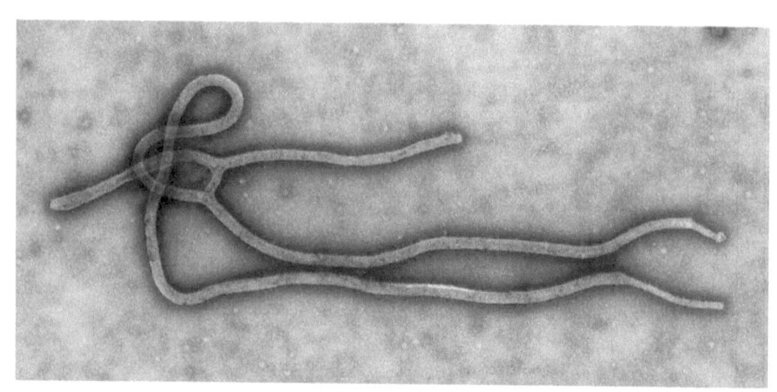

Ebola

Is there a cure
For the unknown,
Breaking us down
Everyone knows.

People are dying
Kept far apart,
In isolation
Touching our hearts.

No one can go in
No one can come out,
For spreading Ebola
Thousands in doubt.

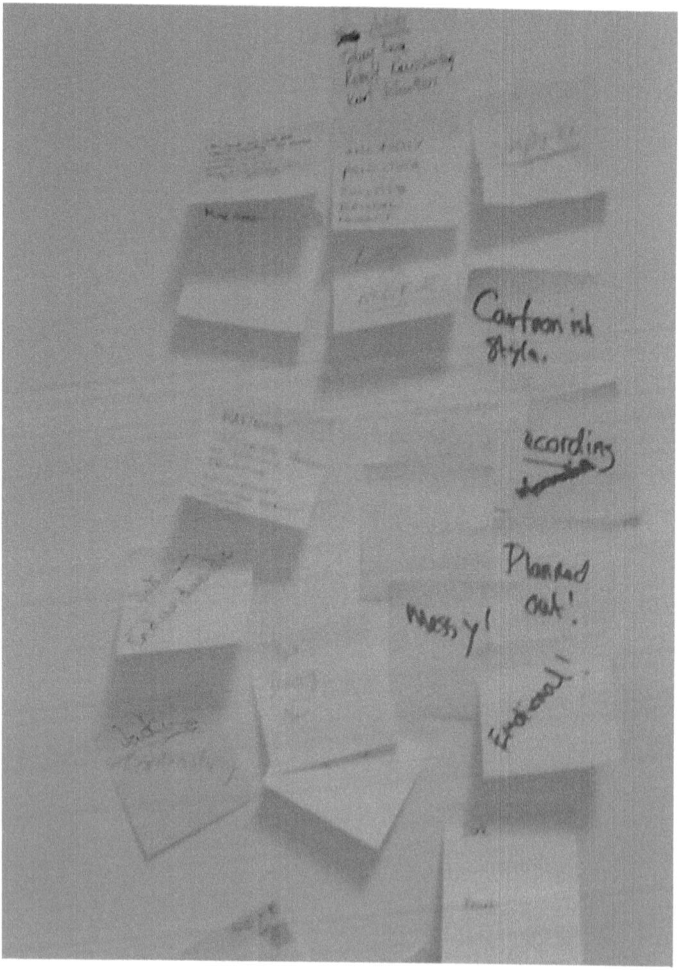
Cartoon ish Style.
Planned out!
Messy!
Emotional!

Coming Out

Our countries at war
Our people gone astray,
Homes torn apart
When can we, say.

We want to be heard
For our rights to live,
Sat on the border
With no one to give.

Freedom is here
We'd like to all shout,
Live and let live
Enjoy our lives, without doubt.

Our children growing up
What is there for them?
Fighting and poverty
A world with no stem.

We are worried, communities
We want a fresh start,
From the beginning
Satisfied hearts.

A Childs Prayer

Cries from a distance
Hidden, we are still,
Buried deep in rubble
A search is on. Our will.

Bombs from somewhere
Dropped in the night,
I was asleep in my cot
They woke me with a fright.

I want my parents with me
I do not know where they are,
Now with unknown people
My memories disappearing far.

I think I have a brother
He was in the room with me,
Blackened smoke was over us,
I hope that he is free.

A normal house we lived in
A garden I did play,
But, now I can't go back there
It is not safe today.

Mother

I wish I could be with you
Each night and passing day,
I was always so proud of you,
In my heart, you will always stay.

Now, I am much older
A Mother just like thee,
If you were only here
If only they could see.

If I could bring back my childhood
We would have our picnics on the grass,
Making daisy chains and laughing
For our closeness would always last.

Sometimes I still smell your scent
I carry it through my love,
Touching it, when I need you the most
My Mother, Up Above.

I wish you could be here with me
To tell me it's alright,
To hold you close, to feel your warmth
To whisper you goodnight.

Moon Walk

A walk along the seafront
On a cold dark night,
The roads are almost empty
But a stream of street lights.

Looking across the seabed
Up towards the moon,
Not a cloud in sight
The stars will appear soon.

Relaxing, just strolling along
Tranquil, it's a delight,
All along the seafront
On a winters night.

Welcome
Manchester
Art Gallery
Free entry
Welcome
Manchester
Art Gallery
Free entry

Unfound Talent

A visit to our galleries
Viewing art, unfound,
From used feelings and emotions
A place for higher ground.

Artists could be distinctive
Within their work they show,
Structures of their Being
All in time they'll grow.

They need our support
Through us they will give,
Breaking out with dignity
Of their views and how they live.

It is interesting, it is useful
Through history that we tour,
Look around our galleries
They are exciting to explore.

Famine

Our third world needs us
Desperate, so very weak,
Charities across the globe
Taking supplies as we speak.

Lots of dirty water
Insects that fly around,
People dying endlessly
The third world on the ground.

Education is getting through
To keep them much more safe,
To guide their population
Further from the grave.

Clothes, food and medicine
Are sent with love and care,
To stop our third world from suffering
To say that we'll be there.

Giving a little every month
If every household could,
To build better communities
For if it was our own, we would.

Time Of The Horizon

As the sunsets, on the horizon
Amazing, beautiful to see,
People gather from all around
For everything it is to be.

Fabulous colours of orange
Fill the sky, so blue,
As we snap shots for memories
From the timing of our moon.

So many different colours
Join this timing sight,
When a flock of birds, go past it
So very slow in flight.

Seeing is believing
A wonderful world so high above,
Showing to us a meaning
From another kind of love.

It glows across the water
So silent through and through,
It brings a warmth inside us
It will always be our view.

Fondest Times

A visit to a favourite place
Fond memories take the path,
Search for a place to sit
Or a picnic on the grass.

Go with friends or family
Make the day worthwhile,
Having fun and laughter
Record photographs in a file.

Changes that have taken place
It is not the same anymore,
No matter how many times you've been
The images are hard to score.

Feelings of the past, that's there
Changes everything inside,
Going home with, emotions
That always get left behind.

Sitting at home
Watching TV,
Curled up on the sofa
With a hot mug of tea.

Wrapped in a blanket
The cold won't come through,
Mind keeps on thinking
For something to do.

Finally, you begin to relax
With no more things at hand,
Switching over channels
Searching for something grand.

At last, at last we find something
But half of its been shown,
Then we still see it until the end
If only we had known.

Feeding

Out for some time
Bread in a bag,
Sit down where it's quiet
The park or lake is not bad.

Grab a few minutes
Look around, where we are,
Meet people we know
How time goes so far.

Take a hold of the bread
Into pieces we tear,
Birds flock around
Kindly we share.

They come from all over
From high up above,
To have our left overs
That we give with love.

Feeding time has gone
Just some crumbs on the ground,
Only a few birds left now
We all leave with no sound.

Seeing

Alarms ring
We look to see

A letter comes
We wonder

The bus is late
We think

A car horn blows
We ponder

www.ingramcontent.com/pod-product-compliance
Ingram Content Group UK Ltd.
Pitfield, Milton Keynes, MK11 3LW, UK
UKHW040020200726
13854UKWH00001B/276

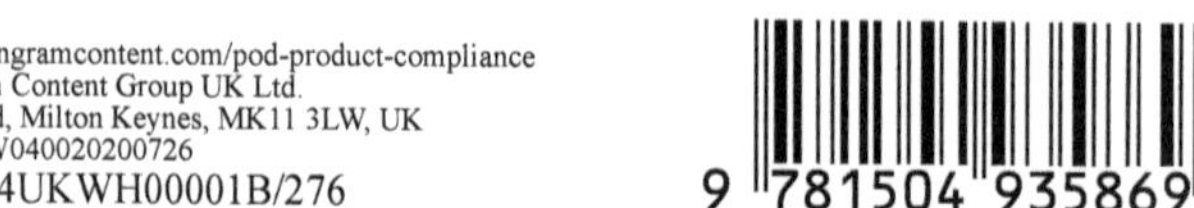

9 781504 935869